In the Street

Gill Tanner and Tim Wood

Photographs by Maggie Murray
Illustrations by Pat Tourret

A & C Black · London

Here are some of the people you will meet in this book.

The Hart family in 1990

The Cook family in 1960

Bill Hart

Linda Hart

Kerry

Lee

David Cook

June Cook

Susan

Linda

Andrew

Lee Hart is the same age as you.
His sister Kerry is eight years old.
What is Lee's mum called?

This is Lee's mum Linda when she
was just nine years old in 1960.
She is with her mum and dad,
her brother and her baby sister.

The Smith family in 1930

Richard Smith

Lucy Smith

May

Jack and June

The Barker family in 1900

Charles Barker

Alice Barker

Fred

Harry

Lucy

Amy and Adam

This is Lee's granny June
when she was just a baby in 1930.
Her brother Jack is looking after her.

This is Lee's great grandma Lucy
when she was six years old in 1900.
Can you see what her sister
and her brothers are called?

3

How many differences can you spot between these two photographs?

One shows a modern street
and the other shows a street
one hundred years ago.

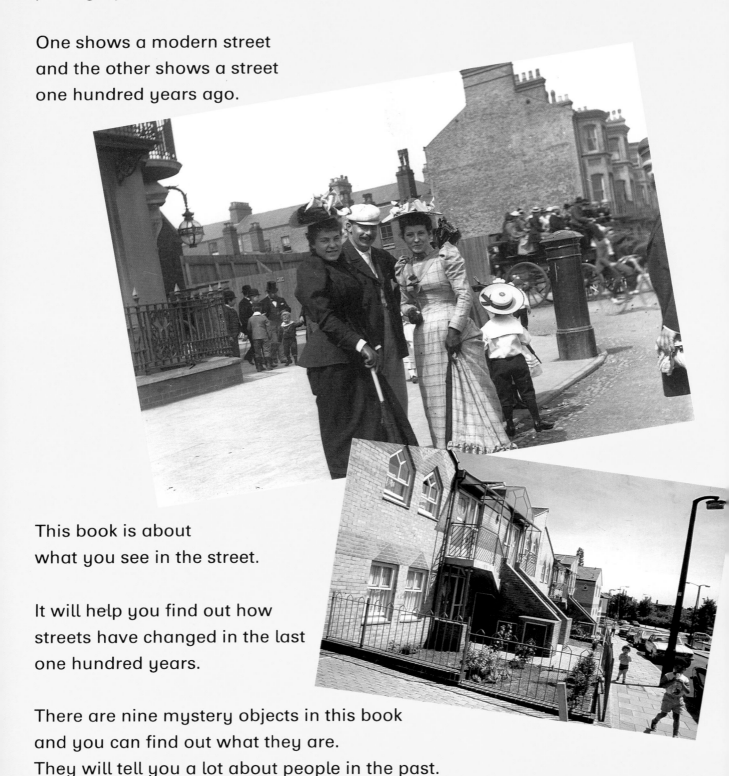

This book is about
what you see in the street.

It will help you find out how
streets have changed in the last
one hundred years.

There are nine mystery objects in this book
and you can find out what they are.
They will tell you a lot about people in the past.

This mystery object stood outside
the Barkers' home in 1900.
It is made of metal.
It is nearly as big as this book when it is open.
It is fixed firmly into a block of stone.
A big clue is that it was used for keeping something clean.
What do you think it is?

Turn the page to find out.

5

This is the street where the Barkers lived in 1900.
How is it different from your street?
Can you find the mystery object in this picture?
It is a **boot scraper**.

In those days the streets
were much dirtier than they are today.
The Barker children have been for a walk in the rain.
They all have muddy feet.
Fred uses the boot scraper
to scrape the mud off his boots.

6

This mystery object is made of metal.
It is the same size as a dinner plate.
The metal plate covers a hole in the pavement
outside the Barkers' house.
What do you think went into the hole?
What do you think this object is?

Turn the page to find out if you are right.

The coalmen are delivering coal to the Barkers' house.
The coalmen take the full sacks of coal from their cart.
They empty the sacks into the coal cellar
through a hole in the pavement.
Can you see the mystery object in the picture?
It is a **coal hole cover**.

In those days many people kept their coal
in an underground cellar.
The coal hole cover was a lid
which covered the coal hole when it was not being used.
The cover stopped people falling down the open coal hole
as they walked along the pavement.

This mystery object stood on the edge of the pavement outside the Barkers' house.

The whole object is four times as tall as you are.

You may have something like this in your street.

But yours will work by electricity.

What do you think it is?

Turn the page to find out.

It is getting dark.
Can you see the mystery object in the picture?
It is a **gas streetlamp**.

ALBERT STREET

A lamplighter lights all the streetlamps
each evening.
The lamplighter carries a long pole
with a hook on one end.
He hooks a ring under the lamp and pulls it
to turn up the gas and light the lamp.

This mystery object stood on the pavement
near the Smith family's house in 1930.
It is made of metal painted red.
The whole object is quite a bit taller than you.
You can see part of it in this picture.

What do you think the letters stand for?
The crown is a big clue.
What do you think the mystery object is?
Turn the page to find out.

It is nearly Christmas.

The Smith family are posting Christmas cards.

Can you see the mystery object in the picture?

It's a **pillar box**.

Jack stretches up to post the letters.

Richard shows May the crest on the side of the box.

The "G" stands for George.

The "VI" is the Roman number six.

The "R" stands for "Rex" which is Latin for king.

Whose name is on the pillar box?

Whose name goes on a modern pillar box?

This mystery object is taller than you are.
It is made of metal.
You can probably see it's a kind of clock.
But this clock does more than tell the time.
Can you guess what it might be used for?

Turn the page to find out.

Richard Smith is taking the children shopping
They are waiting to catch the trolley bus.
The trolley bus is driven by electricity
which it picks up from wires above the road.
Can you spot the mystery object?
It is called a **Bundy clock**.

After the driver has finished his journey,
he puts his own key into a special keyhole
on the Bundy clock.
As he turns the key it makes a mark
on a roll of paper inside the clock.
The mark shows if he is keeping to the timetable.

14

This mystery object is made of wood.

It is twice as tall as you are.

You could get right inside it.

What do you think it is?

Look carefully. The writing will give you a big clue.

Turn the page to find out.

The Smiths are out for a walk.
They have stopped to chat to their local policeman.
Can you see the mystery object in the picture?
It is a **police call box**.

In those days policemen did not have radios.
If they needed to speak to the police station
they had to telephone from a police call box.
Other people could use the telephone
on the side of the box if there was an emergency.
What would you do if there was an emergency?

This mystery object was used by the Cook family in 1960.
It was used by other people in the street as well.
You can see that there is a telephone on the shelf.
But what do you think
the metal box on the right is for?

Look for a button labelled A
and a button labelled B.
What else can you see on the box?
Have you ever seen anything like this before?
Turn the page to find out what it is.

How is this street different from your street
or from other streets in this book?
Can you spot the mystery object?
It is a **public telephone**.

David is helping Linda to make a telephone call.
She puts some coins in the slot and dials the number.
If she gets through, she will press button A
to make the coins fall into the box so she can speak.
If she does not get through, she will press button B.
This makes the coins fall into a cup at the front.
Then she will collect the coins to use again later.
What do you do when you make a phone call?

18

This mystery object is made of metal.

It is about the same size as one page of this book.

It has some numbers and a letter on it.

Have you ever seen anything like this?

You could look for something like this
on a wall near your house.

Do you know what it is?

Turn the page to find out.

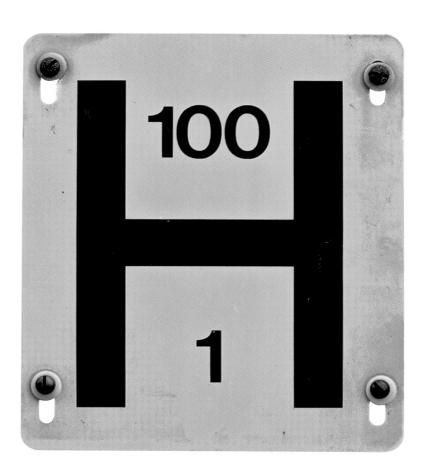

There is a fire
in the street where the Cooks live.
Can you spot the mystery object?
It is a **water hydrant plate**.

The firemen take water from pipes,
called water mains, which run under the road.
The firemen connect their hoses to the water main
using a big tap called a water hydrant.
The yellow plate marks where the hydrant is.
The top number shows the size of the water main.
The bottom number shows how many metres
the hydrant is from the plate.

Now that you know a bit more about streets
and how they have changed
over the last hundred years,
see if you can guess
what this mystery object is.

It was built when Lucy Barker was a baby.
It is made of stone.
The main part is like a big box which is longer than you.
At one end is a statue, a carving and some writing.
Look carefully. You may spot a big clue.
What do you think it is?

You will find the answer on page 24.

Presented by the
Holbrooke
Drinking Fountain
and Cattle Trough
Association

Time-Line

These pages show you the objects in this book and the objects we see in the street nowadays.

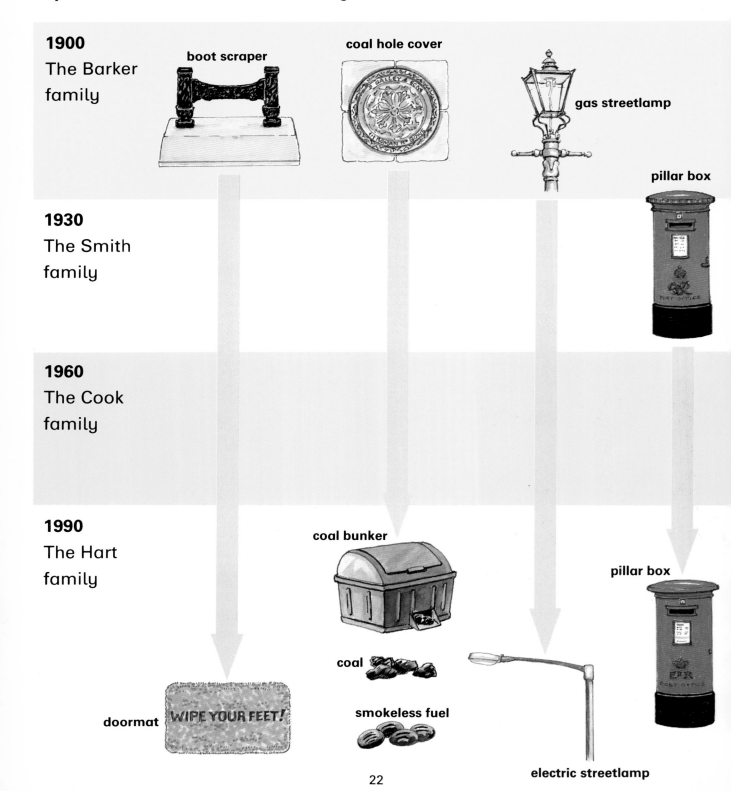

1900
The Barker family

boot scraper

coal hole cover

gas streetlamp

pillar box

1930
The Smith family

1960
The Cook family

1990
The Hart family

coal bunker

pillar box

doormat — WIPE YOUR FEET!

coal

smokeless fuel

electric streetlamp

Bundy clock

police call box

public telephone

water hydrant plate

register

police radio

ticket machine clock

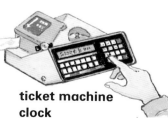

coins

public telephone

telephone card

mobile telephone

water hydrant plate

Index

The **mystery object** on page 21 is a **horse trough**. In 1900 there were hardly any motor cars. Carts, trams and buses were pulled by horses. Some people were worried about the welfare of working horses. They joined together and paid for drinking troughs to be built.

For parents and teachers

More about the objects and pictures in this book

Pages 5/6   The boot scraper was a simple iron blade used to scrape mud from the sol It was an integral part of the entrances to all houses built at or before this time. Streets in 1900 were dirtier than they are today, mainly because of poor surfacing.

Pages 7/8   In 1900, most town houses wer heated by coal fires. The coal cellar was usually at the front of the house, under the pavement.

Pages 9/10   The first British street to be li by gas streetlamps was Pall Mall, in 1807. Brighter electric streetlamps began slowly to replace gas streetlamps after 1881. The gas streetlamp shown on page 9 has been adapted for use with modern gas, and is sti in working order.

Pages 11/12   Pillar boxes were introduced in Britain shortly after 1850. Red became the standard colour for all British pillar boxes in 1884.

Pages 13/14   Trolley buses first appeared 1882. They got their name from the trolley which ran along overhead power lines to collect the current. This system was devise by an American, Leo Daft.

Pages 15/16   The first police call box appeared in 1929. Police radios, fitted to lorries, were first used in 1933. But the police call box remained the main form of communication for police officers on the beat until the introduction of personal radios in the 1960s.

Pages 17/18   The first coin-operated publi telephone box was introduced to Britain in 1906. Payments were made after the call when the operator asked the caller to deposit the correct number of pennies into the box. The first pre-payment box was introduced in 1925.

Pages 19/20   The first municipal water supply was introduced in 1847. The first water hydrant followed a year later.

Things to do

History Mysteries will provide an excellent starting point for all kinds of history work. There are lots of general ideas which can be drawn out of the pictures, particularly in relation to the way streets, street furniture, family size and lifestyles have changed in the last 100 years. Below are some starting points and ideas for follow up activities.

1 Work on families and family trees can be developed from the families on pages 2/3, bearing in mind that many children do not come from two-parent, nuclear families.

2 Find out more about streets in the past from a variety of sources, including interviews with older people in the community, books, museums, old photographs and postcards.

3 There is one object which is in one picture of the 1900s, one picture of the 1930s, and one picture of the 1960s. Can you find it?

4 Arrange a field trip to a museum which has reconstructions of streets from the past, or visit a part of a town or city that is rich in street furniture.

5 Look at the difference between the photographs and the illustrations in this book. What different kinds of things can they tell you?

6 You could build up an archive or school museum of pictures and objects to do with streets. You might like to look for old photographs or maps of the area in which your school is based.

7 Encouraging the children to look at the objects is a useful start, but they will get more out of this if you organise some practical activities which help to develop their powers of observation. You could ask the children to draw pictures of the street objects that they saw on their visit. After returning to the classroom, suggest that one child describes an object to another child, who must then pick out that object from the collection of pictures.

8 On the field trip, encourage the children to answer questions. What do the objects look and feel like? What are they made of? What makes them work? How old are they? How could you find out more about them? Do they do the job they are supposed to do?

9 What do the objects tell us about the people who used them? Children might do some writing, drawing or role play, imagining themselves as the users of different objects.

10 Children might find a mystery object in their own home or school for the others to draw, write about and identify. Children can compare the objects in the book with objects in their own home or school.

11 After returning from their field trip, children might make an exhibition of 'before' and 'after' pictures of different street objects. Talk about each pair of pictures. Some useful questions might be: How can you tell which objects are older? Which objects have changed the most over time? Why? What do you think of the old objects? What would people have thought of them when they were new? What are their modern equivalents? How well do you think the objects might work? Is the modern version better than the old version?

12 Make a time-line using your pictures of street objects. You might find the time-line at the back of this book useful. You could include pictures in your time-line and other markers to help the children gain a sense of chronology. Use your time-line to bring out the elements of *change* (eg. the gradual disappearance of horse-drawn traffic; the increase in the use of motor cars and how this has changed the shape, size and function of streets; how street furniture has changed and developed; how many streets have become too dangerous for play) and *continuity* (eg. we all use streets as thoroughfares; we almost all have our houses, workplaces and local shops on streets).

History Mysteries

First published 1995
A & C Black (Publishers) Limited
35 Bedford Row, London WC1R 4JH

© 1995 A & C Black (Publishers) Limited

ISBN 0-7136-4160-6

A CIP catalogue record for this book is available
from the British Library.

Acknowledgements

The authors and publishers would like to thank the staff
and trustees of the National Tramway Museum, Crich, Derbyshire;
Dan Hyndman; Val Wilmer; Mrs Tanner's Tangible History.

Photographs by Maggie Murray except for:
p.4 (top) Hulton Deutsch Collection; p.4 (bottom) Brenda Prince/Format Photographers.

Filmset by Rowland Phototypesetting Limited, Bury St Edmunds, Suffolk
Printed and bound in the UK by Hunter & Foulis Limited, Edinburgh